Spiritual Revelations

Other Books written by Lynn Lee Bryant:

Peeling Myself a Soul, 2004©

Animalyrics, 2011©

Spiritual Revelations

A book of poetry, short story, and song,
humbly praising Jesus and the almighty God

Written by:

Lynn Lee Bryant

Author of
Peeling Myself a Soul
And
Animalyrics

iUniverse, Inc.
Bloomington

Spiritual Revelations
A book of poetry, short story, and song,
humbly praising Jesus and the almighty God

Introducing:
Terri Lynn Price (walking in love, and release),
and Leroy Watson (Tank's Tale)

iUniverse books may be ordered through booksellers or by contacting:

iUniverse
1663 Liberty Drive
Bloomington, IN 47403
www.iuniverse.com
1-800-Authors (1-800-288-4677)

ISBN: 978-1-4620-3864-0 (sc)
ISBN: 978-1-4620-3903-6 (ebk)

Printed in the United States of America

iUniverse rev. date: 10/27/2011

Contents

prelude

i remember as a child sitting at the bedside of my
grandmother
along with my sisters, singing hymnals.
it was a period of magic as we became absorbed
and relished in the moments.
to this day, i still cherish and often sing
my grandmother's favourite songs.
her favourite religious singer
was mahalia Jackson.
the belief and fear of God was instilled within me
very early.
my mother taught sunday school,
my grandmother was on the church usher board,
and my mother's twin sister sang in the choir
(as did my grandmother).
during puberty, my sister and i would have
to recite bible verses
at my grandmother's home for the children of the
neighbourhood.
we offered free peanuts to those that showed up.
when my mother moved our family
to a better neighbourhood,
she gave our old home to the church.
the blessings of the Lord have always been with me and
my family.
may he be with you and yours?

dedication

this book is dedicated to my family,
those who are living,
and to those who have moved beyond the earthly form.

this book too is dedicated to my special friends
Marlisa and Dossie.
and to all of humanity.
may the blessings of God be upon you
and your treasured soul touched as you read these words.

for love,
for luck,
for laughter,
for life . . .

Lynn

forward

it gives me great pleasure to acknowledge
the hard work of my sister and her effort
in the writing of her third book.

she truly walks by faith and not by sight.
she has my blessings, in all of her ways.

with this new book on spirituality,
by the grace of God,
she has shared with us her blessing
which God has bestowed upon her.

for she has been given the gift of writing
by God, and leaves a legacy for those
who truly believe

Leon Nathaniel Bryant
May 08, 2011

holdz

i'm not sad, not surprised
just beholding,
to the power of the Creator
over my mind . . .

feeling the breeze of His breath
upon my back,
my centre,
my sight . . .
i'm flying blind.

at first it was shock
which i felt,
like stunned . . . numb,
undone.

but as the day went by
ever so slowly,
and i listened to the
thunder in the sky . . .

i realized

why,
and how,
and when,
that just then,
the Lord had come by:

i praised Him.

i promise to always believe,
cherish and entrust,
and
to deliver and receive
His love.

i shall not lie down
in pity
or
drift aloft.

no

GOD is real . . .

no room
left for doubt.

meldin visionz

i feel so Spiritual, humbly blessed
to be realizing my dream,
it's the core of things beneath my wings,

the itch inside my chest
ultimate fear, unrest:
yet pleasure of the mind.

behold . . .
the magnificence of faith

behold
the majesty of the Creator

behold
imagination unrealized

unfold.

the dreams of the Saviour
cruising on and on

engulf the visions
of Jesus
as your own

creative, believing;
blinding and strong.

His children holding
far deep inside . . .

the combination
to the lock
of their life.

powaz

never take the love of GOD
lightly,
for His power is surely
real.

over your own,
your children
breaking all the rules,
self-appointed Authority
to make you kneel.

upon the stomp
of His magnificent feet.
earthquakes and landslides,
volcanoes pouring molten steel.

what's not really yours?
even your soul
can He retrieve . . . ?
if He sees in it evil
or in deceit

He who created
can take away . . .

yes
this force
is really, really
real.

u ready for judgement day?

gerlfrendz

girlfriends
are like therapists,
but do get tired of your flack . . .
they say or do something crazy,
and you have to ask . . .
is there a guardian angle
stuck to my back?!

at times your senses get shocked
no longer to attest,
like a jolt to restart your heart . . .

from cardiac arrest!

at 4am in the morning,
rain at the crack of dawn,
ain't a real friend i know
whose shoulder i can't
call, cry,
lean . . .
fall on.

telling you like it is . . .
getting on your nerves
sometimes
pushing gently . . .
from behind,

me and my girlfriends
a few
with something in common, and kind.

be there when you need them,
even when you think you don't,
and sharing life's experiences since . . .

and you never forget it does first commence.

eldahs

i had one auntie left,
i remember telling others . . . myself . . .
and fear inside;
my fathers only other sibling
just died.

i thought of my grand-pop
sitting on the wooden porch

smoking his pipe.

"it's only i arthur left"
fighting tears he could
not escape.

i flashed back to the photo
my grand pappa carried about,

a long line of handsome folk
in their prime . . .

that one teardrop will forever follow my life . . .
for tonight it is my father's turn to cry
the
very lonesome plight.

my mind has no emotion
my thoughts—not very
clear
shocked,
sad
thinking of my dad tonight,
my thoughts of
here, there and any where.

i know my aunties found her way
just awaiting her new plan;

resting, joyfully anxiously to receive
the Creator of woman and man.

today she joined those gone before
as called by His command;

and humble of the will of thy
Master,
He who has the power at His hand

why not be mine

why not be mine
and live today . . .
and every daaay? . . .

why not be mine
a kiss away?

why not be mine?
humbly . . .
we'll pray.

why not be mine
today,
and always?

i'll be in Heaven
with blue skies above,

i'll hold you tightly
and cradle you
with love.

i'll tell you softly
the words
i've made up

i'll touch you in flight
as we pare as doves.

why not be mine
a kiss away?

why not be mine?
humbly . . .
we'll pray.

why not be mine
today
and always?

might we be humble?
and cherish our time?
might we be humorous?
honouring our life line?

might we create?
a future of favour,
be righteous
in serving,
giving of our labour.

why not be mine
a kiss away?

why not be mine?
humbly . . .
we'll pray.

why not be mine
today
and always?

might we be giving?
choosing those in need . . .

donating time
or a friendly greeting?
why not be mine
a kiss away?
why not be mine?
humbly . . .
we'll pray

why not be mine . . .
today
and always?

halleluiah woo hooo

up up
as we whirl
around
in song
and laughter
and play!

whaaaa
beeeee
hay yaaaaa tah day
whaaaa whoo
halleluiah
halleluiah
halleluiah
halleluiah

woo hooo
halleluiah
halleluiah
up up
Praising my Lord always!!!

trusts of GODs love

GOD
you trust us with so many loves
the love of you, foremost;
that of my family,
as clinging to a dove.

love so resilient
conception so pure,
from the body of a female
placed there by you.

i sometimes think of the loves
of all kinds . . .
how each is different
yet all
are mine.

i think of my mother and father
wise and strong,
yet like fine china,
they treasure me . . .
however, wherever, whenever.
or at your home

looking into their eyes
i see
a vision of me so complete.

i am you see
the offspring of
hours of counting,
of endless love.

i am the creation of Thee.

misjudged

don't take it
out
on me
this jealousy,
or thing . . .

just cause
i'm
there
to get
the phone ring!

drop me out
of your life,
like a dead
bird
from a nest!

think
i can't rest?

upset no
shocked, yes;
at this mess
you tryin to possess!

like a dragon slayers sword
within my heart,
don't judge me,
my
integrity . . .

is sound
profound.

tested true
you lost?
find your own route.

for inside of me
is the
strength
i've worked to achieve . . .
for i believe.

gifts
are bestowed
mercifully.

the Creator's love
gives;
with a servants
glove.

always to care for me
always to share
all i need . . .

feel me?

have fought battles
many, not few

been wounded physically and mentally
from being screwed.
some i trusted
didn't understand . . .

still lately

it's not me,
but they
with issues at hand.

don't take it out on me
jealousy . . .
cause i don't know,
can't guess,
don't care to have,
biased problems integrated
from others . . .

into me,
from elsewhere.
don't judge me,
my integrity.
i've let go
of those things
coming near from others slight . . .
or weakness
or fear
not relating to me
or by my cause
don't judge me
you're on permanent pause.

walking in love

by Terri Lynn Price

step by step
praising my GOD above
with him by my side
i'm walking in love.

from the right the left
and the left to the right
He's watching over me
every day-through the night.

He made the whole world
and rested for a day
Jesus Christ is His name
and it's to Him do i pray!

i may not be perfect
be riddled with sin . . .
have you ever heard the story
of 'daniel in the lion's den?'
He saved him with a miracle
and He can save you too
just praise His Holy Name
and you'll be walking in love too!

natral hie

thought it'd be
lightening
but instead there's this cloud
in my head . . .
should go on
cause I can surely see . . .

the vibrant ray coming thru the cloud
has covered me.

i see life
and i see anew . . .

working hard;
chill-in with a few.

digging deep and
hard and shallow . . .

still from some come words
sharper than an arrow; the straight, negative
and narrow.

the missing:
the absence,
purely not soul
captured . . .

i am
like a ghetto dance . . .
of rock
and
rapture.

birds chirping,
babies stroll,
thugs rapping . . .
ladies hold.
yeah
ain't no hype
this body feels
like a
spirited redbird . . .
spinning on her heels.
like the raindrops
of the Heavens
about to be revealed . . .

child at heart

i 'm a child at heart
in my thinking indeed:

i jump up and down
and whirl around
at the mere sight of an odd tree
or
see the flights of
birds in the sky
passing by,
in War Lord style.

for it is now morning,
and i am happy to be alive.

last night
i saw fireflies,

lights sparkling with a dance at night,
twinkling with inherent unity;
treasures glowing in pitch black.

mo ta va tion

where in the world do you get it
when your get up
done got up and gone?
packed up
left without notice
got up, it just got up
and gone.

didn't know it had done got up,
let alone . . .
got up and gone.

left without notice to home . . .
got up,
done got up
my get up

done got up and got up,
and gone.

gotta call on you once again;
my Spiritual friend . . .

b the staa

it's your life
why not take part?
for if it were a star
with a concert,
and you had no money to go
it would break your heart.

you'd be moaning and groaning
in complete despair,

or if you were going . . .
spending money you don't have,
on clothing and hair.

it's your life,
why not take part?
save those dollars,
believe in yourself;
handle rainy days,
create alternates to sorrow . . .
go with God
He's got all you need to borrow.

dreamz

i know now what to pray for,
my dream . . .
me . . . me!

reality

of being at liberty

to ask questions
to give my heart and soul . . .

to work hard.
to endure, to perceive,
to achieve,

by faith imbedded:
to receive!

this gift of writing,
what i feel, what i see,
what i realize . . .
it's His belief in me.

blu moon

*the moon was encircled
with hints of grey and blue,*

*the grey and blue ringed
by the shades of
of an orange and yellow hue*

*appearing within an array
as it began to move,*

*encased within the clouds
within Heavens view,*

*the darkness was still,
as the moon continued
to appear . . .*

*and i thought i saw a
Heavenly relative there.*

i felt so in tuned

with the environment,

i neglected to see . . .

nature had captivated . . .

and kidnapped me.

stone mountain

the night was dark,
looking over
those skies of stone mountain.

it was fall . . .
mostly brown and red leaves were found.

just a few trees stood tall.
green and crisp,
a few . . .
only losing a branch or two . . .
to the winters frigid mist;
the Heavenly breath,

of mother natures hiss.

parentz

my mother and father

i love them both . . .

but surely know

that GOD as Creator . . .

loves them more.

Heavens' court

there ain't no need
to have a jury
in Heaven.

there ain't no need
to keep a
bailiff on the side.

there ain't no need to record what is said

for all the words were written . . .

when man became a thought,
in God's head.

He wanted me

He wanted me
He wanted me
He wanted me
He wanted me
He wanted me
He wanted me
He wanted me

and i got down on my knees
and i said my thanks to Thee . . .
He wanted me
He wanted me.

my body was so tired
and i got so i would cry . . .

so i prayed to the Lord above,
He accepted me with pure love,
He wanted me,
He wanted me,
He wanted me,
He wanted me,
He wanted me,
He wanted me,
He wanted me,

and i got down on My knees
and i said my thanks to Thee . . .
He wanted me,
He wanted me,
He wanted me,
He wanted me,
He wanted me,
He wanted me,
He wanted me,

for so long i had such pain,
my body had no strength . . .

my flesh felt all so worn,
but my spirit wasn't torn . . .
my mind stayed on the Heavenly dreams;
and the Lord God heard my screams!
He wanted me,
He wanted me,
He wanted me,
He wanted me,
He wanted me,
He wanted me,
He wanted me.

and then He set me free . . .
oh free,
oh Lord,

He wanted me
He wanted me
He wanted me

oh free . . .
oh Lord,

to live with Thee . . .
oh Lord,

He wanted me,
He wanted me.
He wanted me.

my tears woven into welts of pain . . .
my headaches, and my face,
body, cross burning terrain . . .
my chest so—full—of emptiness,

cause i'd nearly forgotten
to celebrate . . .
an essence of myself.

He wanted me.
He wanted me.
He wanted me.
He wanted me.
He wanted me.
He wanted me.
He wanted me.

with GOD's and endless love . . .

through oceaned eyes . . .
i'm not lonely, now realize
it is GOD: the Salvation
the Salvator:
He wanted me
He wanted me.

Lord's forbidden garden

the babe'd been taken
and couldn't tell,

he'd crossed the forbidden creed
of a babe's worst hell.

feeling torn apart,
ripped,
snipped,
stolen and sore
ooohhh . . .
slipped.

never spoke a word . . .
fear from some,
love shone by none.

changed as he aged . . .
indifference beat into his head.

softened,
weakened teen most times
just lying in his bed . . .

never really learned
what a man's supposed to be,

for a man had taken his innocence
from pure and un-jaded he,
just after he was weaned.

couldn't ride a road bike,
wouldn't swim the creek . . .

for at nightfall,
he had to pretend to have recovered . . .
and was one of rosy cheeks.

some ain't born,

some don't spawn . . .

as those that interfered . . .

out of his own infertile lawn.

took one of the Lord's forbidden
creatures:
took his innocence and charm . . .

for that interference
re-infertiled
their own infertile lawn.

blanking

my eyezs never blanked
until time past,
and i was worn . . .

from trying to hard
and forgetting the importance
of myself being born.

my eyezs never blanked
never did we have a date . . .

yet, now that i've moved on
i accept with no regret.

my eyezs never blanked,
now i look back . . . and know

it was a lesson of life . . . so i accept blame of my own

and taking life's lesson,
decided to let go.

neva take fa granted

never take the love of GOD for
granted,

for His power is surely
real . . .

over your own,
your children,
breaking all the rules . . .
self-appointed authority:
to make you kneel!

upon the stomp
of His magnificent feet . . .
earthquakes and landslides,

volcanoes pouring molten steel.

don't take for granted
what's not really yours . . .

for even your soul
can He will retrieve
if He fees in at evil . . .

ill will or deceit.

pastorz

reflected in our society
as a gospel man,

"what's happening now?"
a bible in his hand.

words followed by responses . . .
from the people in the crowd,

going back to the elders and ancestry . . .
rhythmic, jumping, shouting, chime-in in loud!

religion and his culture,
an inseparable pair . . .

critical to his existence,
a part of his daily sacred affairs.

outside of this setting . . .
listening to a speech anywhere,
call and response emerges . . .
cause it's always been there.

creative expressions, raw:
revealed in the norm,

ideologies of life itself,
pure expression . . .
cultivated in art form.

self revelation,
tranquilizing your soul . . .
hand—clapping spirit!
call and response unfold.

moans and groans
begin to emerge . . .
                natural and pure
you are now,
          as you once were . . .
without words.

servantz of Christ

i don't care whether
mary was married to Jesus,

why would it matter to me?

for i only care . . .

that she loved
the Saviour of my life . . .

and only wish i lived then,
and there.

i'm not surprised
she was at the
side of my Lord,

as a woman . . .

as a believer,
as a saint,
for women have been
there forever and a day . . .
propelled through blinding
and unwavering faith.

nine lives

i'd sometimes heard
the cat has nine lives
but never found it in books,

then i saw "mels movie"—"the Passion
of the Christ"

and witnessed the Saviour
tortured
with a
club of nine stringed iron hooks.

He lived through the
torture . . .
bared my sins
painfully there;

hooks and tails . . .
like a Bengal tigers nails.

His body rendered helpless
fleshless and bare

the taking of His life,
His mother looking on . . .
there . . .

by taking a stand,
through pain,
degradation and strife,
His grandeur to be forever celebrated . . .
by most:
in His brand new after-life.

berth ii

i only heard,
never saw,
the brand new infant,

within the manger
protected by straw.

a north star above
"david" did tell . . .
of wise men three
under the infants spell.

frankincense and myrrh,
oils of the earth,
given by three kings . . .
celebrating the newborns birth.

i heard of a little drummer boy,
striking the drum . . .
till worn tiny arms,
hands, fingers, and thumb worn to nearly numb.

Mary the Babe's Mother
witnessing a miracle,
though which afterwards . . . She

sat humbly cradling,
Jesus had just come . . .
to be.

prayerz

i know now what
to pray for . . .

my dream
me . . . me . . .
reality.

of being free,
to ask for . . .
work hard:
to endure
to perceive
to believe . . .

by faith and kindness, to.

for the gift
of writing,

what i feel, what i see,
what i realize, what i believe,
for my self, my family, my friends
my animals,
and prayer for any enemy.

and for those who refuse to believe . . .
that by faith and kindness . . .
He saved me.

soulz dreamz

a soul has to keep a calendar,
each time an image of
Him
appears anywhere . . .

He has to be lead and be aware . . .
of every path
there.

a soul has to recognize

conflicts which occur,
a soul needs to be active

when your heart
is unsure.

bohrn

it started with the alpha, omega was told,

of a son born—the Lord . . .

on a night

which they say was cold.

they went on to say

a true alpha,

a new philosophy . . .

a new beginning

for all of mankind to be cleansed . . .
and sin free.

Perli Gatez

you may join with others,
block;
embedded in stone,
beneath some rock . . .

the man asked
"my dear Lord why?"
when the lifespan now is some
seventy years nigh?

the Lord replied
"that might be so,

but you tried sneak-in in . . .
so you got a million or more.

the choice was yours
made by you,
you thought you tricked ME?
tried sneak-in in to Heaven . . .

trying to deceive ME."

"on earth you sinned,
you actually asked for a wish"

your wish was as granted,
yet, you tried to sneak-in . . .

finding one thing for real!
I AM the CREATOR;
and judge . . .
of all mankind,

STILL!"

"a million plus years
shall your time be so,

and when it's over, you may apply
for a trip to eternity . . . or more.

for your wicked soul, and not changing your ways . . .

remember it is
I

with control
of YOUR days.

Blessed

i feel so Spiritual, loved, humbly blessed . . .
to be realizing my dream,
it's the core of all things
beneath my wings,
the itch inside my chest.

ultimate fear,
yet pleasure of the mind,

behold . . .
the magnificence of faith.
behold . . .
the majesty of the Creator,

behold . . .
imagination unrealized even by myself,

unfold.

the dreams of the Saviour
cruisin on and on,
i'm feeling freer . . .
the Saviour has heard my sound.

by second, minute, day,
dusk and beyond . . .

engulfing the visions
of Jesus,

as my
own:

creation;
ultimate, believable,
blinding,
safe and strong.

grandma's luvs

i remember
lying in bed,
with the pillow
on my side, just by my head . . .

my heart beating fast,
a little
bit of
magic . . .
can't seem to rest.

the sight of my two babies . . .
lying on my
grandma's chest.
a miracle
but no surprise . . .
as grandma continued to celebrate,
the gifts of her life.

the three would be snoring . . .
face full of ice cream,
sleeping so hard,
wouldn't hear me if i screamed.

i loved to see
the trio rest,
instant pita-pata: in my chest.

creation rightz

i want to
move toward
creation rights
the way it appeared eldridge did,

soul always challenged, but cleared.

to see man as more than himself,

the image of he, as only GOD could have made
and a will to be . . .

from human, to environment, to one of
all living things.

i vividly imagine how it would be
to see the river nile,

a river flow upstream;

with such an imaginative beauty . . .

mankind has rarely seen.

momz and popz with GOD

comforting to know they're in GOD's hands
for it is He who decides
who goes where, how and when
there were no rights.

for two days,
no stars in the sky

yet He kept the visual safe.

the moon was cast so ever high
the ambience peaceful . . .

everything connected in life.

He reclams

barn houses rooted with trees
abandoned sometime ago.

watching the roof and doors
other things through awed curiosity.

food for the termite and other animals
however minute, to feed.

mysteriously enchanting, strong the century streets.

the driveway to the house, about a half a mile away
is really a forest
a road carved of clay . . .

there were no lights, no place but greenery,
or so it seems,
the house had changed into a planter.

plants heartily growing through the sinks, windows
doors, and floors,
the home returning to earth, with fungi and mold.

Lord's ladi

i heard my mother call me
"hey lynn"
and saw her
so clear . . .
i knew GOD the Father
had sent her spirit here.
she had on white,
called me a few times,
let me know;
she is absolutely fine.

the picture, the voice
so crisp, visibly clear

placed me in a blissful moment . . .

no stars in the skies

piercing black darkness,
that fails
even the sharpest of eyes.

release

by terri lynn price

Lord is this pain
my trial?

this emptiness—this loneliness.
it clenches at the throat

every song has a meaning—
i . . . miss . . . you . . .
i . . . want . . . you . . .
i hate myself for loving . . .
you . . .

what have you done to my soul?
i already know—
taken half and made it . . .
your own—

give it back—not fair . . .
hurts . . . so . . . much.
where are you?

give it back me

everything used to have
meaning . . .

i . . . miss you . . .

tankz tale

Leroy Watson

well known as worldwide,
bout to grab my microphone,

i'm gonna reveal my life,

in the life i live . . .
my thing in life is being in the Lord.

my thing is i roll i lie . . .
one day for sure i know i will die.

this is a real world—is what
we see everyday,

what i see is hate harm . . .
everybody trying to live the rich man way.

the only thing i can see is me,
that's one of the only thing i see,
cause GOD gave me a chance,
and i m gonna take it for me.

kept moving on,
stayed strong,
had faith . . .
had time.

gotta give it up
turn it loose,
like james brown said . . .

love my family and friends,
let them know
i love them,
and need them . . .

but GOD is the only way in which it can go.

pickelz and grandma's calm

time passed quickly one stormy rainy night.
the moon and stars were absent;
the sky was dark
with thunder and lightening strikes.

pickles, aged 6, jumped, scared by sight and sound.
her hair and shiny pink night gown glowed,
as her eyes searched around.

she lay there afraid and silent
not cracking a smile.
she then remembered
grandma had made her a special hair style.

her plats were 7 twisted,
with ribbons,
silver and gold buttons applied.

she grabbed her head
and took a twist apart,
pointing it toward the absent stars
her fear started to fade,

as she saw and heard her grandma say,
"its ok child,
it's always been this way."

"the rain provides us water,
and GOD claps his hands . . .
making thunder.
the brightness is his surprise.

close your eyes my child,

for He's trying to tell you,

He's just passing by".

rain

rains boldly coming down
ever so light
or in with a stormy night

hot most times on the equators throne,
cold down here this far
from Mother Natures home

black haired beauty
from the west side of town
strong
persevering woman
for heart string songs

she's got her share of life
those hazy, dazy ups
those lazy crazy downs
creeping up
when no one's around.
she prays to the Father, singing Heavenly phonics,
enchanting sounds of faith, and glorious harmonics.

why man?

of all the animals
man is the single that enjoys injecting pain;

goggles and clothing to protect identity,
of the hunter's anatomy,
to himself pleasure . . .
by his own measure.

you said you were my friend,

yet you sent me into a lion's den.

to let you know
i am not rude,
just telling what i know.

you are not my friend . . .

you are a lost soul.

lisnin

there is no simpler manner
in how she likes
to live her life.
talking to nature
facing one step, one step,
at a time.

listening to nature, birds singing
the feeling that
they sang as one,

in unity.

giving me this
empathy,
for all,
and
the lisnin.

lady lizard

lady lizard
asleep,
lying by a tree . . .
awakened,
unaware
of what she was,
or wanted to be.

she saw a snake
crawling in the grass,
saw it feeding,
decided for herself . . .
in that position
she wouldn't last.

saw a bird
flying in the air,
decided for herself
too much of a scare . . .

saw a frog
leaping around,
thought about it closely . . .
would rather be on the ground.

saw a human
walking on two,
looked at her body . . .
noticed she could walk and run
on two, too!

she had no idea
she was a lizard,
saw nothing
resembling herself,
as though she had come from no where . . . and going
nowhere else.

she prayed to God, and placed her burden on him:
Father where am I? where am I supposed to be?

with chest held high, and tongue hung low
she took a deep breath of life, as she wanted to know.

she took a bold step:
and moved away from the tree,
and noticed the grass provided a path,
a gateway she previously did not see.

she wanted to find something . . .
anything . . .
that would help with her identity.

she moved very slowly,
through the path, looking all around,
dodging water puddles and debris . . .
newly discovered ground.

she then ran fast,
then faster indeed . . .
for she wanted to know
what and who in the world
was she?

over and up,
around and about . . .

all of a sudden,
she could hardly restrain . . .
she saw something that reminded her
of her family's terrain.

for in the grass

and greenery of the yard . . .

she heard her mama sing.

she ran so fast, this time on two,
and found her happiness . . .
the one she once knew.

momz and popz love

i can feel their love
in the places
which i know,
in these spaces:
there are no faces . . .
memories come and go.

love was abundant,
fresh . . .
and forever new.

still within the sparkles
of
silver and blue . . .

i mostly think of Heaven
God
and you.

He knew it was me

He knew it was me
Yeah!
He knew it was me
Yeah!
He knew it was me . . .
He knew it was me.
way up in Heaven
He knew it was me.

i started calling His name
and praising the same . . .
my flesh joined;
as my feet moved insane.
my arms started waving,
my hands clapping,
my spirit and body
now one in the
same.

i said,
i love You,
i need You,
i just got to
have You
in my life.
i worship Thee . . .
my Guiding Light.

He knew it was me
yeah!
He knew it was me
yeah!
He knew it was me . . .
He knew it was me.
way up in Heaven
He knew it was me.

i reach for you, and know you're there,
awaiting my turn . . .
knowing my Heavenly Blessings,
could appear
from anywhere.

He knew it was me
yeah!
He knew it was me
yeah!
He knew it was me . . .
He knew it was me.
way up in Heaven
he knew it was me.

voicez in the shadowz

i've come a long way
from the shadows,
cause i praised
the Lord out loud,

it is He whom i applaud . . .

i've come a long way
through the shadows,
cause i said the words aloud.

i've come a long way
from the shadows,
cause i asked him
with my voice . . .

i've came a long way
from the shadows,
cause the Lord gave me a choice.

i've come a long way
from the shadows,
cause i praised
the Lord out loud,

it is He whom i applaud . . .

i've come a long way
through the shadows,
cause i said the words aloud.

i've come a long way
from the shadows,
cause he heard
my words and cries:

I've come a long way
from the shadows,
cause the Lord heard me . . .
His child.

i've come a long way
from the shadows,
cause i praised
the Lord out loud

it is He whom i applaud . . .

i've come a long way
through the shadows,
cause i said the words aloud.

praising Jesus
and calling His name,
asking him

to tighten my Yoke . . .
for i need him
in this life's game.

i've come a long way
from the shadows,
cause i praised
the Lord out loud,

it is He whom i applaud . . .

I've come a long way
through the shadows,
cause i said the words aloud.
calling out loudly,
and asking for help,

with this voice
He gave me . . .
and thus i was kept.

i've come a long way
from the shadows,
cause i praised
the Lord out loud,

it is He whom i applaud . . .

i've came a long way
through the shadows,
cause i said the words aloud.

the sun's rays
shine lightly
about me.
as He showed me my new life . . .
in dreams,
i know joy comes in the morning . . .
cause Jesus answered me.

i've come a long way
from the shadows,
cause i praised
the Lord out loud,

it is He whom i applaud . . .
i've come a long way
through the shadows,
cause i said the words aloud.

i love ya,
i love ya Lord,
i praise you,
i praise your name . . .
i need you,
and will call on Thee,
for You have set me free.

i've come a long way
from the shadows,
cause i praised
the Lord out loud,

it is He whom i applaud . . .

i've come a long way
through the shadows,
cause i said the words aloud.

Bless you Lord . . .
Halleluiah,
Halleluiah,
Halleluiah,
again . . .

i worship you Lord,
i honor your reign,
i thank you very loudly,

dear Lord . . . for alleviating
the greatest of my pain.

i've come a long way
from the shadows,
cause i praised
the Lord out loud,

it is He whom i applaud . . .

i've come a long way
through the shadows,
cause i said the words aloud.

ta nite

i watched the moon
in the sky

tonight,

dark, black, grey
jagged clouds . . .

passed ever so gently by.

a slow steady roam,

changing, moving and gliding,

in the permanent

Heavenly home.

life's blood

my life, His life
His word my bones,
His flesh my nerves . . .
His soul my bloodstream,
i pray to earn.

i cry,
for God made each,
bread and wine taken,
of the blood and flesh . . .
of one so fresh . . .

Jesus, such pain he felt . . .
all from non-believers,
today,
still being dealt.

His arms my yoke,
His teachings, my breath,

for if not for Jesus . . .
there'd be nothing left.

no replacement,
only God and Jesus to care,

for it is my God and Jesus . . .

Who's always and forever there.

suzy lu–2

i shook and trembled,
my stomach contracted in a knot . . . tight.
my head hurt,
my eyes and face swollen,
oceans of tears running down my face . . .
i kept calling her name,
"suzy-lu", mah . . .
my body ached.

my soul cried out!
there was this lifeless feeling,
as though i were alone
in the world . . .
i felt afraid,
i felt a void,

i prayed . . .
and gave the Lord
the burden to take.

the tears continued to flow,
even then;
as i wrote.

the missing of my mom,
to the Lord . . . my secret prayer,
provided me a serenity,
for i knew she was in His care

for i had a heart-wrenched mind . . .
after you moved;
my suzy-lu:
to Heaven's shrine.
i had not the strength . . .
during that transitioning time.

then my eye lids felt as wings,
bringing my body behind,
for all i saw in thinking of my mom.
my mind constantly sensing her,
her spirit . . . to touch me
come see me, always in Heaven's time.